AF270353

Soybean Crops

by Grace Hansen

Abdo Kids Jumbo is an Imprint of Abdo Kids
abdobooks.com

abdobooks.com

Published by Abdo Kids, a division of ABDO, P.O. Box 398166, Minneapolis, Minnesota 55439.
Copyright © 2024 by Abdo Consulting Group, Inc. International copyrights reserved in all countries.
No part of this book may be reproduced in any form without written permission from the publisher.
Abdo Kids Jumbo™ is a trademark and logo of Abdo Kids.

Printed in the United States of America, North Mankato, Minnesota.

052023

092023

THIS BOOK CONTAINS
RECYCLED MATERIALS

Photo Credits: Alamy, Getty Images, Shutterstock, United States Department of Agriculture

Production Contributors: Teddy Borth, Jennie Forsberg, Grace Hansen
Design Contributors: Victoria Bates, Candice Keimig

Library of Congress Control Number: 2022946719
Publisher's Cataloging-in-Publication Data

Names: Hansen, Grace, author.

Title: Soybean crops / by Grace Hansen

Description: Minneapolis, Minnesota : Abdo Kids, 2024 | Series: Agriculture in the USA! | Includes online
    resources and index.

Identifiers: ISBN 9781098266202 (lib. bdg.) | ISBN 9781098266905 (ebook) | ISBN 9781098267254
    (Read-to-me ebook)

Subjects: LCSH: Crops--Juvenile literature. | Agriculture--Juvenile literature. | Farming--Juvenile
    literature. | Field crops--Juvenile literature.

Classification: DDC 633.3--dc23

Table of Contents

The Miracle Crop

Soy is the second largest crop in the United States. It is sometimes called a "miracle crop." This is because it has many different and important uses.

The History of Soybeans

Soybeans are a type of legume. They are native to China. The crop came to North America in the 1760s. By the 1950s, the US was the largest soybean exporter.

7

Soybean Farms

Today, there are more than 300,000 soybean farms in the United States. Most can be found in the Midwest region. Illinois, Iowa, and Minnesota are the top growers.

Minnesota
Iowa
Illinois
soybean farm

There are different kinds
of soybeans. Most soybean
farmers in the US grow yellow
soybeans. Yellow soybeans
are used to make soy milk,
tofu, and other products.

More than 70% of soybeans grown in the US feed livestock. Chickens, pigs, dairy cows, and beef cattle all eat soybeans. It is their most important **protein** source.

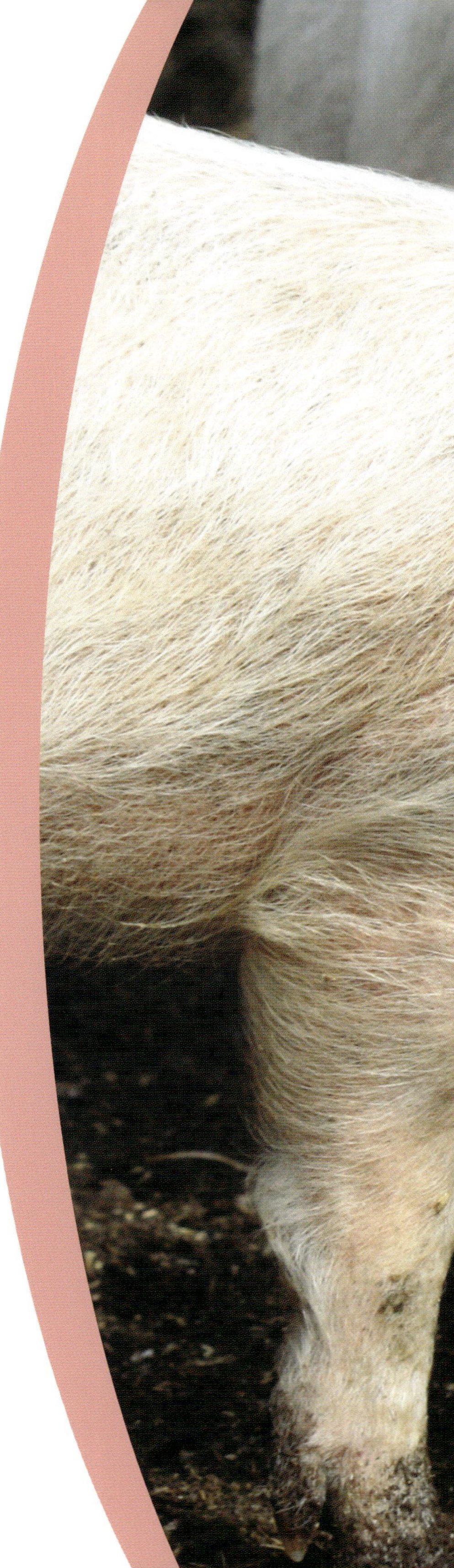

13

In late winter, when the soil is warm enough, farmers begin the growing season. They choose the best seeds for their soil. In the spring, they plant each seed 1 inch (2.54 cm) below the ground.

By fall, the soybean plants are fully grown. Their leaves turn brown and fall off. The pods are exposed. The fields are ready for **harvest**!

17

After **harvest**, the beans
are sold to a grain elevator
facility. There, they are
stored safely. Then they are
sold to a **processor**.

Soybeans can be processed into many different products. This includes food ingredients, soy foods, and industrial products.

Parts of a Soybean Plant

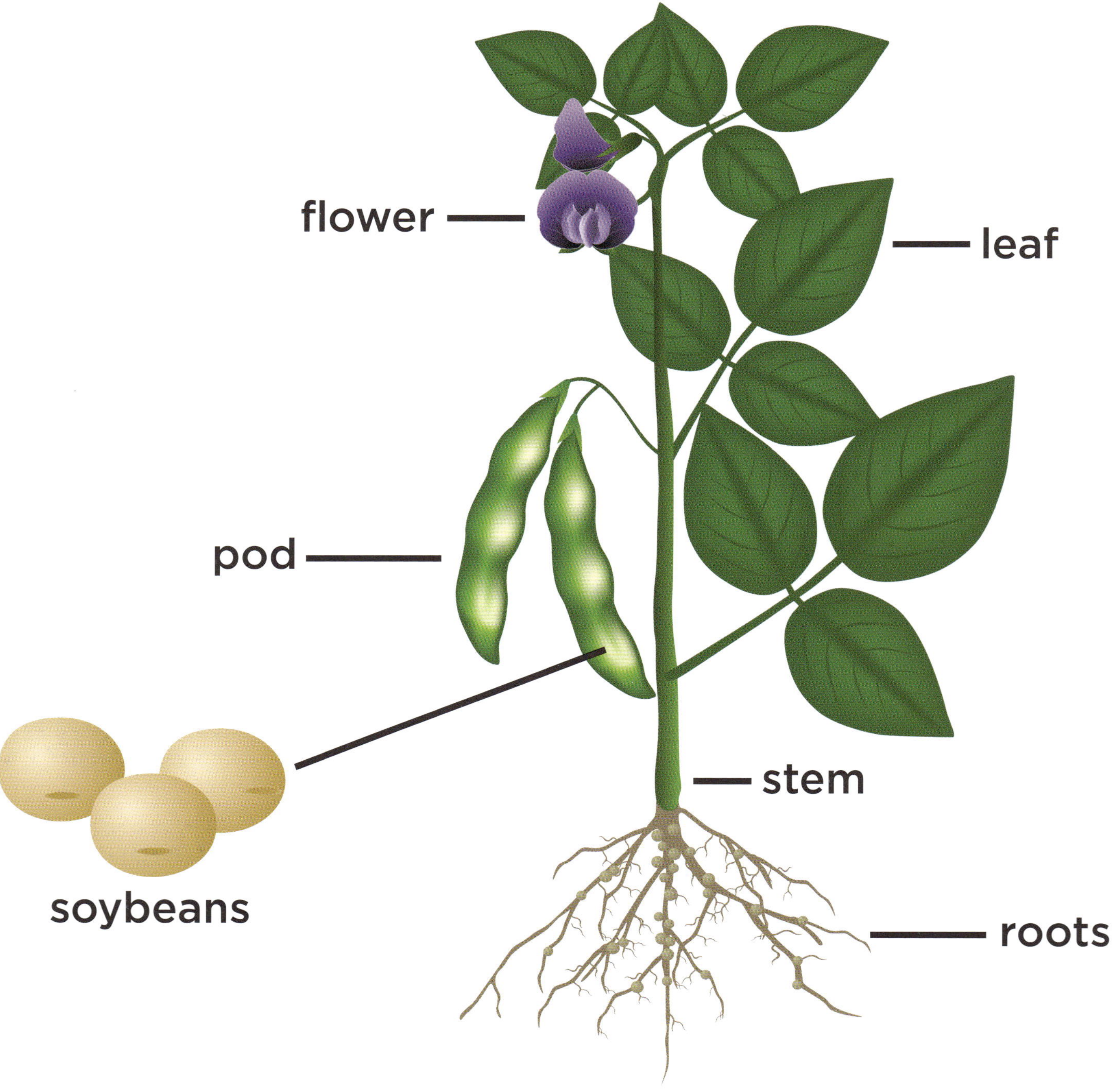

22

Glossary

exporter – a country that sends goods to another country to sell.

harvest – the gathering of ripe crops, the crops or the amount of crops gathered, or the season in which they are gathered.

legume – any of the family of plants that grow their seeds and fruits in pods. Beans and peas are legumes.

native – a plant naturally found in a given place.

processor – a company that prepares and processes food for humans to eat or into other products.

protein – a substance made up of certain elements that is found in all living things and is a necessary part of life processes.

Index

Visit **abdokids.com** to access crafts, games, videos, and more!